Donal Neary SJ

COMMUNION REFLECTIONS
FOR
SUNDAYS AND HOLY DAYS

YEAR B

VERITAS

First published 1996 by
Veritas Publications
7-8 Lower Abbey Street
Dublin 1

Copyright © Donal Neary SJ, 1996

ISBN 1 85390 340 X

British Library Cataloguing
in Publication Data.
A catalogue record for
this book is available
from the British Library.

Cover design by Banahan McManus
Printed in the Republic of Ireland by Betaprint Ltd. Dublin

CONTENTS

Introduction 5

Season of Advent 7

Season of Christmas 11

Season of Lent 20

Season of Easter 28

Ordinary Time 40

Holy Days 79
    The Immaculate Conception 79
    The Epiphany of the Lord 80
    St Patrick 82
    The Ascension of the Lord 84
    The Body and Blood of Christ .85
    The Assumption of Mary 87
    All Saints 89

INTRODUCTION

Communion Reflections for Sundays and Holy Days of Year B presents short reflections, mostly based on the scripture of the day, which are suitable for reading after communion. Sometimes the reflection is centred on the feast of the day or a general aspect of the Christian life, for example, the reflection for the Feast of the Immaculate Conception is a prayerful meditation on Mary. Now and then a general reflection has been used.

Many people have noted that the Mass can 'end very suddenly', and there is need for a wide variety of reflections which may sum up and link in the readings, theme of the feast and the Mass. They value highly the inclusion of a Communion reflection, read in the quiet time and space of the Mass after Communion has finished, not while people are on the way to Communion.

On reading the Communion reflection

In introducing people to reading the Communion reflection, some attention might be paid to the differences between reading meditations, praying a prayer, preaching a homily, proclaiming the Scripture.

A Communion reflection is to be shared, rather than proclaimed or preached. This affects the tone of voice, the mood communicated through reading, the speed of reading and the way of preparation. It will be read slowly. In cases where some line of the Scripture is repeated, two voices might be used. Repetitions of words will be noted, as they then sink into the heart. 'Gently', 'softly', 'prayerfully' and 'slowly' are words the reader of the Communion reflection might recall when reading and preparing to read.

Careful preparation is more necessary for Communion reflections than for other liturgical readings, which may be more familiar. The Communion reflection is new both to reader and listener, and thus needs careful and prayerful preparation. The reader of a Communion reflection should have the text well in advance of a liturgy and have time to pray over it.

Many people find the use of music in the background to Communion reflections intrusive. Others find it creates a mood of reflection. If music is used in the background, it needs to be such that does not distract from the reflection. Thus, an instrumental played too loudly or the music of a well-known hymn can distract from the content of the Communion reflection.

Communion Reflections For Sundays and Holy Days of Year B may also be used for private prayer; many of the reflections might be used also on other liturgical occasions, fitting similar themes or Scripture readings. May they enhance the liturgy with personal reflection on the great mysteries of our faith and thus bring the reader personally closer to the Lord Jesus, whose death and resurrection is the theme of every Christian liturgy.

Donal Neary SJ

FIRST SUNDAY OF ADVENT

Being faithful

Be faithful to God and God's presence in life.

Because of God there is always hope.
everything is being created all the time:
the star you see is bright each night with new light,
the love you share with another grows stronger,
and living friendship reaches deeper into the soul.

Every Christmas is a new creation,
and the old, old story is told again,
with new gifts, new carols,
to friends old and new,
among people who have always been part of life,
among people who are new this year,
and among people who are sharing Christmas
this year in the eternity of God.

All is new:
be faithful to hope,
be faithful to the future,
be faithful to God who is among us.

Among us like
the raindrop on the grass,
the warmth of winter sun,
the touch of a friend,
among us like a child,
vulnerable, new and eternal
like a child.

Be faithful in waiting,
that God might always be new.

SECOND SUNDAY OF ADVENT

Prepare the Way of the Lord

The weeks of Advent prepare for Christmas;
all we associate with Christmas prepares us for Jesus,
for his birth in the love of Mary and Joseph.

All of us can be like John the Baptist,
preparing a room for Jesus Christ in our families,
among friends, in schools and workplaces,
preparing a room in our hearts for love.

Or Christmas weeks can be like empty tinsel;
singing the songs of Christmas and forgetting the birth,
or playing Santa and pretending love;
or being so busy that you wish it was already over.

But it need not be like this.

Allow time these days for prayer,
for moments taken in a busy day,
like stopping in the heavy traffic,
and just remembering that Jesus is near.

Take time for friendship, for love, for care,
for those activities that grow our friendship and love
with the people who mean a lot.

Take time these days for the poor,
for ensuring that someone's Christmas
will be better
because of your generosity.

Then the songs will be full,
and gifts will be reminders of love,
and Santa, the friend of children,
will be like the Christ-child.

Then love for God and others
will come to birth at Christmas.

THIRD SUNDAY OF ADVENT

Witness for the light

>May my life speak as a witness for the light;
>
>where there is darkness may I bring light,
>where there is loneliness, may I bring companionship,
>where there is pain, may I bring healing.
>
>May my words bring comfort to others,
>as the morning dawn lightens the darkness,
>and may my prayers bring hope to others,
>as the moon gives its light to the city.
>
>May my touch lighten
>the loneliness and fears of young and old,
>and may my sufferings and struggles,
>as these were part of the life of Jesus,
>and part of the life of Mary and Joseph,
>bring hope and depth to others.
>
>And when like the Baptist, I cry,
>in the wilderness of anxiety, fear and hopelessness,
>may I be heard by God
>and may the light of Jesus
>lit in the love of Mary and Joseph,
>shine through the ways I deal with pain,
>and comfort the pain of another.
>
>May I believe
>that each person,
>like John the Baptist,
>is a voice speaking the word of God.
>
>May the way of Jesus Christ,
>Prince of Peace, Son of God,
>be bright in my soul and the souls of others.

FOURTH SUNDAY OF ADVENT

Yes!

When Mary said 'yes' to the Incarnation,
she said yes to God and promised
that she would centre her life
on God's invitation to be the mother of his Son.

She said 'yes' to new life,
she said 'yes' to faith that God would look after her,
she said 'yes' to trust that God would not let her down,
she said 'yes' to hope that her son would find his way in
    life;
and isn't all this like any mother or father,
as they await new life?

She said 'yes' to her questions
about pregnancy and about marriage,
and did not expect easy answers;
as the mist takes hours to rise over the hills,
as the river takes days to return to its level,
as both dawn and darkness slowly mature,
she would be patient with life and with God.

Did she not think of this 'yes' to her trust in God
when she heard of her cousin's pregnancy,
when she found no room in the inn,
when she watched Jesus being rejected,
and when she stood at the foot of the Cross?

If we say 'yes' to faith, to hope and to love,
If we say 'yes' with thanks and with trust,
If we say 'yes' to God's grace in our lives,
we will never be alone.

CHRISTMAS VIGIL

The mingling of God and his people

> When you mingle scented oil with water,
> you find a lovely fragrance.
> The fragrance of the plants, the roots,
> the scent of the ingredients of the oil.
>
> And if you had only oil without water,
> the fragrance would be overpowering.
> It would smother you, take away the breath of life.
> And if you had only water without oil,
> well, you'd have no fragrance, no depth,
> and you'd not notice anything new.
>
> Something the same with God and ourselves.
> Christmas is the mingling of God and of us.
> He mingles with us in Jesus Christ,
> a baby born in the ordinariness of the womb,
> the way we all become human.
> A man like us, one who would suffer and die,
> and be raised from death.
>
> He is God and one of us.
> Without Jesus God is too heavy,
> all-powerful, awesome, remote,
> the judge and controller of life;
> like oil with no water.
> And the beauty, power and fragrance of God would
>   overpower us,
> like oil overpowers on its own.
> With Jesus we more easily believe that
> God is love and compassion and involved with us.
> Without God Jesus would be not worth our life's
>   following.
> Just a man, a big leader, dead and gone,
> a man of earth, of time, created like one of us.

God and his people mingle in Jesus,
the baby-God,
the teenage God,
the adult God,
the risen Lord of all.

Praise to the Lord who comes among us,
glory be to the Father from whom he comes,
glory be to the Spirit whom he sends,
Glory be to him,
the mingling of God and his people,
in Bethlehem,
through all ages,
and now among us.

CHRISTMAS DAY

And the word was made flesh and lived among us

In the ordinary, the Lord was born.

A child born for us,
a son given to the world;

son of Mary, born of the Holy Spirit,
and within the love of Mary and Joseph.

Jesus, like all of us, needed to grow up,
in the environment of love.
His growth from childhood to adolescence,
from adolescence to adulthood
took place within the usual human way;
learning from experiences,
studying his religion,
formed like all of us by family and neighbourhood,

within the love of Mary and Joseph,
within a village community, and an extended family
of cousins, aunts, uncles, grandparents.

He celebrated his parents' birthdays,
he looked after them when they were sick.
He went to his grandparents' funerals,
and later watched at Joseph's death
and consoled his widowed mother.
A young man growing up
and feeling all the joys and struggles of life.

He learned about God from the Bible,
and worshipped every sabbath.
God became man in a very human way.

Doesn't this enhance our humanity?
Doesn't it show the worth and the dignity of us all?
God really mingled with us in the birth of Jesus.

Mingling among us
like light and earth mingle to grow the tree,
like memory and love mingle to keep friendship alive,
like water mingles with wine for drink for our journey,
God and humanity one in Jesus Christ.

And the word was made flesh and lived among us.

FEAST OF THE HOLY FAMILY

Every family is holy

> Family roots go deep:
> the first lessons of love and trust,
> the first experiences of belonging,
> of acceptance and of joy
> were in the family.
>
> In the quarrels and misunderstandings of the family,
> we learn to forgive and be reconciled,
> and we know that it is a place
> we can always return to.
>
> Family gives us a place in the family of peoples,
> and family makes a small corner of the world a home.
>
> Jesus grew up
> as we all grow,
> in the family and love
> of Mary and Joseph.
> In the family
> he learned to love
> and allowed himself be loved.
> And his family watched in love
> as he endured the struggles of life,
> and his mother was with him to the end.
>
> Family is never perfect;
> whether two-parent, one parent,
> whether there are divorces or separations,
> we live within the love and weakness of a family,
> within all the human fragility of relationships,
> and it is there we grow as people,
> like branches from the root of a tree,
> like the shoots and petals on a flower,
> like the fruit and food from the earth.

We are created in the image of the family of God,
Father, Son and Spirit;
we watch as Jesus, Son of God, Son of Mary,
grew to maturity in his extended family;
and each family,
like Jesus, Mary and Joseph,
from the grace of God
and within the love which founds the family,
is a holy family.

SECOND SUNDAY AFTER CHRISTMAS

The Lord is near

In the moments of life
when we need care beyond the ordinary,
and in the ordinary cares,
God is near
in Jesus,
the light of the world.
In admitting our need for God,
God is near.

In the moments of life
when others need God
and approach us in their needs,
we feed them
with the word of God,
the bread of life,
with Jesus,
who came among his own,
the Word made flesh.

We need God,
in our cries to him,
we feed God,
in our service to others.

The child who is helpless and nourished by love,
the quarrelling couple healed with forgiveness,
the lonely person enlivened by friendship,
all are fed by God,

for God is near
in the love and care of others.

Homeless, poor, abused,
victims of greed,
helpless in illness or depression,
the Lord is near.

Home-care helpers,
counsellors and social workers,
people unravelling confusion and hopelessness,
and the bread of life is given.

The Lord is born
when at any time
we bring love to birth.

BAPTISM OF THE LORD

Jesus, our brother and friend,

> born like each of us,
> of a woman, and in weakness,
> plunged himself into human life
> at the waters of the Jordan,
> at the beginning of his life with us,
>
> Into the depths of sin, love,
> into the mystery of fragility, weakness,
> and into the history of his people.
>
> The waters of the Jordan
> are the waters of joy and sorrow;
> they are waters of hope and mystery;
> and they are the waters of sin and division.
> Into the waters of life Jesus plunged
> and made of them the living water of God.
>
> All life is holy, sacred, eternal
> because of Jesus.
> We plunge with him into the depths
> of our own being;
> in the depths of love we will find the God of love,
> in the depths of sin, the God of compassion,
> in the depths of weakness, the God of strength,
> in the depths of division, the God of reconciliation,
> in the depths of poverty and misery, the God of justice,
>
> and in the depths of our humanity
> we will find the divine life of God.

FIRST SUNDAY OF LENT

Jesus was tempted by Satan

We allow ourselves this day
to feel the courage of Jesus.

He had the courage to continue faithfully
what he had just begun -
the work his Father gave him to do.

And to remember the poor with love
in every decision he made.

His was the courage to lead his life
in such a way
even though he knew it would lead
to rejection and to death.

Often we are tempted
to give up on what is good,
to live lives of shallow hopes,
shallow relationships and shallow cares,
and we know that when we want to do something good,
another whisper or strong voice
suggests something else.

Then the Lord is near;
do we not need others in life
to encourage us in the good we want?

Can we allow Jesus,
the one who conquered his own temptations,
to encourage us in our efforts
to remain true in love to what is right?

SECOND SUNDAY OF LENT

Listen to him

> In all times of life,
> we can find hope and new life
> from the word of God.
>
> In the confusions of life
> we find meaning in listening to Jesus.
> In the pain of life,
> we find consolation in listening to Jesus,
> and hearing his words to others like us.
>
> Words like,
> *Do not be afraid,*
> *I am with you always,*
> *come to me all who are weary.*
>
> And when we want to know how to
> shape the commitments of our lives,
> we listen to his words to his disciples –
> *Come, follow me,*
> *Take up your cross and follow me,*
> *Go teach all nations.*
>
> And when we look into the future
> and wonder about life and death,
> wonder about the future for our children
> we get new life from his words,
> *Trust in God and trust in me,*
> *Your heavenly Father will care for you.*
>
> And when we look at the needs of the world,
> at the poverty and homelessness,
> at the debts of the poorer nations,
> at the violence between groups of people,
> we are challenged and inspired by his words,
> *What you do for others, you do for me,*
> *Love one another as I have loved you.*
>
> **This is my Son, the Beloved,**
> **Listen to him.**

THIRD SUNDAY OF LENT

True religion

A prophet once said that true religion
means to act justly,
love tenderly
and walk humbly with your God.

Religion can be a means of
praising God
or serving self,
of service to others,
or caring for self.

It can diminish people,
make them guilty always in the sight of God,
and then it misses the first grace of any faith:
that God loves each of us,
a love that dwells within us
as real as the blood in our veins
the muscles in our limbs,
the hair on our head.

Religion can keep the poor more needy,
encouraging an unthinking acceptance
of the inequality among people.
And it misses then another grace,
that we are brothers and sisters,
and all we are given is for the service of others.

Jesus was angry in the temple,
because of the greed of the sellers,
who were exploiting the poor in the name of religion,
(for the poor had to buy there
the ingredients of their sacrifice),
and mocking the house of God.

And God is angry when people are
exploited,
used,
abused,
in any way –
physically, emotionally, spiritually.

God asks us in Jesus
to share his anger
when in his name
people's dignity is diminished,
or love is abused,
or the poor are exploited
or when he himself is neglected.
This is true religion:
to act justly,
love tenderly
and walk humbly with our God.

FOURTH SUNDAY OF LENT

That we may not be lost

    To be lost is a frightening experience,
    like a child losing a parent in a big shop.
    Maybe losing direction in marriage or a job,
    losing health, good looks, life itself.

    When we're lost we need a signpost,
    or some way of finding direction.

    Jesus is our way, our direction,
    our signpost through life to God.

    He is lifted up;
    so that in every dangerous experience of life,
    we can see him, our risen Lord on Calvary.

    In illness or depression, we know his presence,
    in poverty and injustice, we know his care,
    in mourning and loss, we know his compassion,
    in our efforts to ease the pain of others,
    we know he is with us,
    we are his hand, his heart, his love today.

    He is lifted up,
    never out of our sight,
    for God gave his only Son
    so that we might not be lost,
    but have eternal life.

FIFTH SUNDAY OF LENT

A Lenten prayer

    My God, I love you,
    with love not born of yearning
    For reward.

    No, Lord.
    Rather am I overwhelmed
    That you hugged me to your heart upon the cross.
    The nails, the spear, the searing shame,
    sorrow, anguish, shattering stress,
    and death itself –
    All this you bore for me,
    For me in all my sin and sorrow,
    anguish and shame.

    How could it be that I should love you not?
    Most loving Lord!

    Put aside all prize or punishment of any sort,
    You sweep me up in love and
    breathless I can only say,
    I love you, Lord,
    And I will love you always –
    love my king,
    My very God. Amen.

                                      Prayer of St Francis Xavier

PASSION SUNDAY

Walking on wounded feet

The crowd cheered him,
'Blessings on him,' they roared,
waving flags of palm,
'for he comes to us in God's name.'
And a few days later they cheered again,
this time for his death,
and blessings on a public robber, Barrabas.

A fickle people.
We wonder why?
What changed them?

Like Peter later,
they would say,
'I don't know the man',
for the man they saw later in the week
was, in their eyes, a different man.

The king had become a spectacle,
bloodied, mocked, rejected.
Who wants a leader like that?

Jesus didn't want acclamation,
he had been trying to say all along
that he was a different type of king.

And so he chose a donkey,
as his chariot.
They saw their own hopes
for a leader who would overthrow their oppressors,
and didn't see the real Jesus.

The leadership of Jesus has lasted longer
than any of the public leadership of the time,
because he was king of love, compassion,
and walked the way of his cross –
carried by his wounded feet and the help of a friend,
and guided by the hand of God his Father.

EASTER SUNDAY

Joseph

I'm Joseph, the man who owned the tomb.
I watched the crucifixion of Jesus
with most of his friends
from a distance.

You might say I often felt I was dead in myself,
hanging around the edge of the crowd with him,
asking questions with Nicodemus.
Jesus didn't seem to mind that –
come close when you want to,
no pressure –
was the impression he gave,
and I feel closer to him now.

Life was privileged for me,
no big problems,
enough money and family connections,
but it was very dead.
I'm like people who have never forgiven themselves,
or who are too scared to love someone,
or who find it hard to feel with another person even when
    they want to,
or who thought that Jesus would ask too much.

All he asked of me was my tomb,
and I'm glad now to be rid of that.
I loved my security, in life and death –
I planned where I'd be buried,
and sure, I lived my life half-buried
in laws and fears and whispers of joy.

Now I feel born again,
refreshed by the water of his side
like the water of a womb.

I knew when I gave that tomb away,
I was getting back the gift of life.

Then I was the owner of a tomb,
now I have been gifted with the fullness of his life.

SECOND SUNDAY OF EASTER

Doubt no longer but believe

Don't we find it difficult sometimes to believe in ourselves?
Maybe we haven't been praised or liked as a child,
perhaps we've failed in relationships or jobs?
Or failed in sports, exams and what we've set our hearts on?
And then the change when someone believes in us,
or when things go well, or we can forgive ourselves.
Jesus believes in you –
he loves you and believes in you;
and then he says as he said to Thomas:

Doubt no longer but believe.

Faith in God can weaken.
Once nourishing our life,
it can threaten our happiness.

Once simple, it can become complicated.

Life's tragedies and problems
can take us away from God,
and faith itself finds its own pathways.
The strength of our faith fluctuates,
and we may move from God.

And like Jesus for Thomas,
God looks for us.
Through the locked door
of disappointment, resentment, guilt,
confusion, boredom and let-down,
he comes with peace.

He simply looks at you,
sees into your heart with love,
and with compassion says
to you, as to Thomas:

Doubt no longer but believe.

THIRD SUNDAY OF EASTER

From darkness to light

In all the Easter work of Jesus,
he led the disciples
out of darkness into light,
out of sadness into joy,
out of isolation into community,
giving the living bread of hope
for the dry bread of their disappointment.

He did this by sharing himself with them,
sharing the scripture that spoke of him,
and the bread that was his body.

No long instructions,
no long exhortations,
just the openness
of sharing himself with them.

This is his plea to us, his Church:
be light in darkness,
be joy in sadness,
be community in isolation,
be Eucharist to dry bread,
be wholeness to broken life.

FOURTH SUNDAY OF EASTER

And these I have to lead as well

    Did the Lord Jesus know
    about you and me as he spoke these words?
    And these I have to lead as well.

    You and I are men and women
    in a long line of Jesus' followers.
    His death was for us,
    his risen life is for us,
    the love and compassion
    of the shepherd for his sheep
    is his concern for you and me.

    Like a mother giving extra time to the sick child,
    like a father introducing a child to the world,
    like friends getting to know the real other,
    like all the best relationships in life,
    Jesus cares for you and me,
    as he cared for each of his disciples.

    And he leads us –
    his word is a lamp for our steps,
    his bread is food for the journey,
    his blood is energy for the miles we travel;

    and as the apostles led others to his guidance,
    each of us in our chosen life's calling
    lead the people we know and love
    into the way of Jesus.

    There are other sheep I have
    which are not of this fold,
    and these I have to lead as well.

FIFTH SUNDAY OF EASTER

I am the vine, you are the branches

    I am the river, you are the water,
    I am the mountain, you are the soil,
    I am the love, you are the touch,
    I am the mother, you are the child,
    I am the fragrance, you are the rose;
    we belong with him, and in him.

    There is no river without water,
    no mountain without soil,
    no love without touch,
    no mother without child,
    no fragrance without a flower;

    The risen Lord,
    faithful promise of God to all of us,
    is the source of all life.

    May we be grateful for the gift of life.

    The risen Lord is the source of all love;
    may we be grateful for the gift of love.

    It is a continuous gift:
    the vine gives life to the branches,
    the river gives direction to the water,
    the touch gives the comfort of love,
    the soil is enriched by the mountain,
    the rose is made sweet by the fragrance.

I am the vine, you are the branches.

SIXTH SUNDAY OF EASTER

That my own joy may be in you

>We search for joy and love in life:
>in our emptiness and our yearnings,
>our hurts and our griefs,
>our loneliness and our boredom,
>we want joy,
>and we want to be loved.
>
>And in friendships and loves,
>in the moments of peace and harmony
>among family and with friends,
>there are glimpses of joy and of love,
>and we know that the human heart
>is made for joy and love
>that is everlasting.
>
>Let's be thankful:
>for the joy and love of life,
>for the joy and love of children,
>of husbands, wives and family;
>for the joy and love of friends,
>of neighbours and of colleagues,
>and for the joy and love
>we shared with those who have gone before us.
>
>And let's be hopeful
>in times where all this is missing,
>that it is not missing forever.
>When love is hurt or joy is muddied,
>let's be hopeful
>that we will find such joy again;
>and let even the ache for joy and love
>remind us of love and joy that lasts forever:
>the love and joy of God.

SEVENTH SUNDAY OF EASTER

Consecrate them in the truth, your word is truth

Jesus speaks
of generosity in a world of greed;
of justice in a world of oppression,
and of community where there is isolation.

He highlights the struggle of good and evil,
in the city we live in and our country,
in the heart of each of us.

Where there is bitterness, he encourages forgiveness,
where there is poverty, he asks that we share,
where there is sickness, he asks for patience.

He speaks the truth of the human heart;
of the yearnings in his followers
for equality, justice and reconciliation,
and prays that we may be committed,
consecrated,
to this truth of his heart.

Consecrate us:
may we live for his truth
like the waves reach for the shore,
like the river moves to the sea,
like the rain enlivens the earth,

and like people in love live for each other.

**Consecrate them in the truth,
your word is truth.**

PENTECOST SUNDAY

Breath of the Spirit

> The wind is cool, soft,
> and rises off the sea.
> Touching water and earth
> the yellow of the gorse,
> the mud of the shore
> with gentle movement.
>
> It caresses
> hands,
> head, feet
> and whatever of the body
> is open to its touch.
>
> A breeze,
> gentle, loving,
> who knows from where it comes,
> and where it goes now to touch another.
>
> It touches another,
> the gentle breeze of God,
> made new by touching
> face, hands and feet,
> earth, water and sand.
>
> Breath of God,
> wind of the Spirit,
> word of the Son,
> blow where you will,
> and the world will be renewed.
>
> Word of God, be renewed by human words,
> human life, be filled with the life of God.

TRINITY SUNDAY

And the word became flesh

> The mountain road beckoned,
> and the snows were majestic.
> Peaceful, far away, beautiful,
> the mountain of God.
> Like Father, Son and Spirit
> in strength, beauty, power.
>
> Beckoning the pilgrim,
> challenging the walker,
> strong and faithful,
> and we are afraid.
>
> We call God a mountain and a rock,
> strong, beautiful, yet weak,
> for the rock splits
> and the hills may turn to dust,
> for Jesus, God and one of us,
> one of the Trinity of love,
> is sent among us.
>
> Strength becomes weakness,
> rocks grow flowers,
> snows melt
> and God is near.
>
> Mingling within his people,
> like melting snow in a field,
> like leaves of oak falling to earth,
> for the power of God
> took tiny flesh
> in Mary's womb
> and she gave birth to Emmanuel,
> God is with us.

Jesus, Saviour of all,
friend of the earth,
friend of all people,
God among us.

And now the mystery of God
is no longer a strange mystery,
but a hand of friendship and forgiveness
which each of us may hold forever.

And we need no longer be afraid.

SECOND SUNDAY IN ORDINARY TIME

Where do you live?

>The question
>of the disciples to Jesus –
>Where do you live? –
>is the search for God,
>the quest for truth, love and meaning.
>
>And you ask it sometimes in peace;
>you sit by peaceful water or rushing waves,
>or in a quiet room,
>and wonder without worry.
>
>Or you hold a hand and know you are loved,
>and you live in the world of love,
>and you wonder in joy at the source of it all.
>
>Or you struggle with loss and hurt,
>or with loneliness and confusion
>and the question hurts
>and you wish it would go away.
>
>And the question leads
>to meaning, to truth, and to love.

Come and see:
be prepared to be surprised
by beauty, joy and peace,
by courage and by strength.

Come and see:
be prepared to be open to the love of another
so that it can change you.

Come and see:
and you will know that God lives,
and you're glad to ask the question:
Where do you live?

THIRD SUNDAY IN ORDINARY TIME

Follow me

    We follow Jesus, like the Twelve,
    because we are drawn by him;
    drawn and attracted by the way
    this man Jesus
    lives, speaks, suffers, dies and rises.

    Something in him appeals;
    maybe it's the wish to heal,
    or his love for the poor,
    or his forgiveness, so total,
    or his desire to change the world,
    or because he stands for what is good:
    for justice, peace, equality.

    Or just because he is a friend,
    and because he is
    the face of God, the word of God,
    the son of God.

    Like us, in all but our sin,
    one of us, son of God,
    and son of Mary too.

    People left a lot to follow him,
    they left their dreams and their burdens,
    their families, and their businesses,
    and gave up their lives,

    drawn, attracted, challenged
    as we are now,
    by his words:
    Come, follow me.

Trust that these words draw you, attract you,
trust that these words
are worth the whole love of your life,
for they are loving words of God.

FOURTH SUNDAY IN ORDINARY TIME

And his reputation spread

    They talked about him,
    about the things he said and the way he said them,
    about the people he healed and their confidence in him,
    about his gentleness and compassion,
    and the loving way he talked about his Father.

    Some people liked one quality, others another.
    Some liked his smile, others liked his touch.
    Some liked the new way of looking on religion,
    and others liked the challenge in his message.

    And some did not like him –
    the people who wanted to cheat the poor,
    or oppress people with harsh religion;
    and people were guided by evil,
    by greed or abuse or by sin,
    heard about him, spoke badly of him,
    cursed him, told lies about him.

    Nobody was unmoved by this man.
    His voice reached everyone,
    his care for the poor, the lowly, the neglected,
    challenged the powerful and encouraged the weak.

    What have you heard of Jesus?
    What attracts you?

    Be glad that you love him
    be glad that you follow him,
    be glad that his reputation has spread to your life.

FIFTH SUNDAY IN ORDINARY TIME

That is why I came

    Many times Jesus wondered
    why he was on earth.

    He knew and believed deep down in his Father's will
    that he would live and die and rise for love;
    that he would show the world that God cares
    especially for the poor and the needy.

    And as he preached and prayed
    and healed and forgave
    in the name of God his Father,
    he was a man committed to his mission.

    We want that ourselves:
    to have a place in the world
    where we make a difference;
    where we can love and be loved,
    where we can share life with others.
    We want to ease the lot of the sick,
    to make a difference in the poverty of the world.
    to create a better world for our children.

    Like Jesus,
    we want to know why we are here.
    His conviction
    of why he came
    can touch us.

    For all of us, like Jesus,
    are here on earth for the same reasons:
    to live in the love of God,
    to bring that love in the ordinary places of life,
    and to give praise to God in heaven.

SIXTH SUNDAY IN ORDINARY TIME

Rejected by many, accepted by Jesus

A person rejected in society
came to Jesus,
and openly knelt before him to be healed.
the leper was an outcast;
people feared he would contaminate them.

This illness was a way of defining him;
and then he was put out of sight.

Labels for people define them and narrow them.
We don't want to be labelled.

Maybe we label people out of fear,
or for a quiet life.
If we think they are different from us,
we don't have to deal with them.

Jesus sees the whole person.
not any single part of the personality.

And Jesus was so compassionate, so open
that people couldn't take it,
and he stayed outside the town,
the place where rejected people live.

He was at home there
because he himself was rejected by his own;
he was at home there,
because he touched those people with love;
he is always at home with love.

SEVENTH SUNDAY IN ORDINARY TIME

Your sins are forgiven

We need to hear these words;
when we feel guilty over things said or done,
when our faults are like a dark window,
or like muddied water,
we need these words of Jesus,

Your sins are forgiven.

Like the paralysed man we need others
who will bring us to the forgiveness of God,
who will carry us in the weakness of our soul
when our convictions seem so fragile.

Then the words of Jesus,
Your sins are forgiven,
like melting snow in winter,
like flowers growing from rocks,
like the touch of someone who is loving.

Forgiveness brings joy and freedom,
like when a person is healed
or like when the burden of guilt is lifted,
like a gift we know we need
but which no one can give but God alone.

If we bring our sin to God,
the words of Jesus
will lift our hearts in hope and joy.

Your sins are forgiven.

EIGHTH SUNDAY IN ORDINARY TIME

Thirst for joy

Like a river searching for its way to the sea,
we look for many types of happiness.
The heart and soul in each of us
hungers and thirsts for joy.

We are happy with the beauty of the world,
our successes and achievements,
or the love we have shared in our lives.
And there is a happiness that only Jesus can give;
always in the present moment.

Life with Jesus means a direction in our lives,
not clearing up our confusions
but spreading eternal love among us;
Life with Jesus means a call to work like him,
and to base our lives on what is fullest:
love, friendship, justice, compassion.
Life with Jesus gives a meaning to our lives,
which neither joy nor sorrow can cancel.

We rejoice in the Lord,
glad that we have found faith,
amazed that he has found us,
and loves us every day.

NINTH SUNDAY IN ORDINARY TIME

He stretched out his hand and it was better

We carry with us burdens of the past,
like a river carries its mud to the sea,
or as a house which sheltered us well lets in the damp.

All of us are beautiful and strong at times,
at other times weak and mixed up,
carrying past experiences through our lives.

This is the heaviness within us,
or the fear that blocks us from loving freely,
or the anxieties in face of the future
that make us doubtful and lacking in hope.

People came like that to Jesus,
for healing, hope and freedom.
Like the man with the withered hand,
we bring the withered parts of ourselves to him

for healing,
forgiveness,
strength,
because he has promised this.

Be open with the Lord and you will be healed,
be genuine and you will be strengthened,
be your real self with him
and you will find him a healing Lord in your life.

Stretch out your wounds to the Lord and you will be healed.

TENTH SUNDAY IN ORDINARY TIME

Who are my mother and my brothers and sisters?

> We live our lives in the circle of many relationships,
> connections, friendships, loves.
> We live in a web of relationships
> which have been essential to our lives:
> people close to us now,
> people who have died,
> people who were once part of life
> but from whom we have drifted.
>
> And we live in the circle of God's love.
>
> Maybe we wonder how central
> to our whole lives our special people are.
>
> What can be more central
> than family relationships?
> Yet Jesus says that our relationship with God
> is more central.
>
> We are united in human bonds
> of parent-child
> brother-sister
> and other family relationships;
> that beautiful web of support and comfort
> we all want, hope for and try to give;
> but there is another bond –
> our deepest unity is in God.
>
> As well as our human bonds,
> we are children of God,
> and living within the love of the gospel,
> we are brothers and sisters of Jesus.

ELEVENTH SUNDAY IN ORDINARY TIME

The Kingdom of God grows slowly

The first steps any of us make
are faltering and slow.
It takes time to learn to walk,
and our first words are unclear,
just mumbled sounds.
It takes time to learn to talk.

The Kingdom of God grows slowly,
according to Jesus,
and often we don't notice its growth.

Within each of us
the kingdom of God grows.
Its qualities are
compassion and courage,
forgiveness and faith,
hope and harmony,
peace, joy and love.

As we need patience with learning
in our first words and first steps –
for these are skills learned gradually –
we need similar patience
as God's life grows within us.

And patience with others too;
as we watch a child learn to walk and talk,
we rejoice in the small successes,
we watch with love and encouragement.

Can we have the same patience with
the increase within us and others
of the Kingdom of God?

And the increase of the Kingdom of God
is the growth of love,
and the increase of love among people
is the growth of God within us.

TWELFTH SUNDAY IN ORDINARY TIME

Do not be afraid

Storms of life – which of us hasn't had them?
About exams and jobs, in marriage and friendships.
And our fears of things going wrong.

What sort of fear does God calm?

The fear of being rejected by people close to us,
or the fear of love being lost.

One of the worst things about death
is the fear of being nothing.

Or of losing God,
like when Jesus was asleep in the boat.

You might have had some experiences like that.
Where God saved you.
A big relationship breaking up, a child dying,
a marriage ending,
redundancy or unemployment, alcoholism –
surviving with some happiness even when money was low.

The Lord is close to the broken-hearted –
maybe you knew that at tough times
when you didn't go under and
you knew that God was there.
Be not afraid, for I am with you.

THIRTEENTH SUNDAY IN ORDINARY TIME

Walking free in God

    The girl, once dead and lifeless,
is given new power and new life by Jesus.
She is to walk free.
His word is for us to do the same.
Bring life to each other.

Raising the dead –
this story is untrue to life –
people are dead when they're dead.
It's more the promise of eternal life
and the hope of Jesus to bring comfort to sorrow.
Jesus is giving a big example that he came to bring life.

Ways we have been helped in bad times.
Ways in which we find the right person at the right time.
Miracles are like kindnesses people do for each other
from their love and care and thoughtfulness.

Jesus brought life to a house of sorrow,
but not by himself –
he brought Peter, James and John;
and any time he wants
to do the work of God,
he brings his followers,
he brings you and me.

Be a life-giver;
the person who works those small miracles.

Then Christ works through you.
Then his words are in action and in reality.
Walk free in the love of God.

FOURTEENTH SUNDAY IN ORDINARY TIME

What is this wisdom that has been given him?

We say about someone we know well:
Sure he's one of our own.
One of our own; a sure way of saying we're proud of him –
but we won't take him so seriously.

That's what they were saying about Jesus in Nazareth.
And others said the same: Can anything good come out of
    Nazareth?
Small-town boy with big-time dreams.
How could he have any wisdom: Sure we know his sisters, his
    cousins.

And that's where he got his wisdom,
the wisdom each of us shares.
Wisdom comes through ordinary people.
We know we get some of our wisdom from our family.
We pick up wisdom with the homemade scones out of the oven.
That's how it is.
One of our own.
Maybe you've given more wisdom than you thought.

The wisdom of Jesus is never too complicated.
It's things like: if you want to be happy, see what you can give
    to others.
That's how he saw happiness, and that's the full wisdom of
    Jesus.
He saw it at home – in Nazareth, and he saw it in heaven.
Places of love.
We live by the wisdom of love, rather than by other wisdoms –
like the happiness that comes from straight As in exams,
or from our job, money, or physical appearance.

Real wisdom is to be in touch with love in your life,
and if you're in touch with love, you're in touch with Jesus.

FIFTEENTH SUNDAY IN ORDINARY TIME

Sent out in pairs

In the centre of our lives,
of every day and week,
in work and in the home,
we live in a circle of our relationships.

We know that problems are diminished
and burdens lightened,
by sharing them with another.
Decisions come more easily when we talk them over,
suffering is lessened by the comfort of another.

And whenever we meet
in the name of Jesus,
in the name of love,
in the name of justice,
he is with us.

To preach his word,
he sent his disciples in pairs,
for we do not live our faith alone.

Like a river gathers its fullness
from the smaller rivers flowing into it,
we grow in faith from the faith of others.

In prayer together,
in sharing struggles of faith,
in helping another in sorrow,
in gathering together to work for justice –
whether in pairs or larger groups,
we are engaged in the work of Jesus,
the one who worked with and sent others
on his work of God.

SIXTEENTH SUNDAY IN ORDINARY TIME

Be kind to yourself

    How hard we can be on the person closest to us –
hard on ourselves.

    We all need a bit of compassion for ourselves,
for our weaknesses, faults and failings.
We also need to be able to forgive ourselves –
if we're hard on ourselves, we'll be hard on others.
We can be so hard on ourselves that we're tough on everyone
    else.
Can we accept ourselves as the people we are?
That's having compassion on ourselves.

    We can be hard on ourselves at all ages.
For not being good enough,
failing to reach impossible standards,
for having feelings like jealousy or envy.
And regrets:
Everything you wanted to happen and it didn't.
 Maybe ways you let down a husband or wife, or ways you
    failed your children.

    Jesus was big on compassion. And we need it.
Look on our whole selves : not just one side of ourselves.
If you have harmed people and they forgive you, allow
    yourself be forgiven.
And let the compassion of Jesus give you sympathy for
    yourself.

    We need to love ourselves.

    Accept yourself – love yourself as you are,
not as you might have been
or might be.
Be kind to yourself and you'll be kind to others;

let others be kind to you and you'll be kind to yourself.
Be compassionate to yourself and you will be to others.
Allow others be compassionate to you,
and you'll look on yourself with love –
and that's how God looks on you.

SEVENTEENTH SUNDAY IN ORDINARY TIME

He fed the crowd

    A mother and small child stood in line for communion;
    the child was too young for communion
    so just trailed up by the hand.
    And then looked up at the minister
    with a big open mouth.

    And the gospel came alive
    with the need of the people for food,
    and mouths open for the bread of life.

    The image of this child
    is an image of the gospel,
    as Jesus feeds the people.

    The gift of the bread of life is
    about being open and being fed;
    people hungry from their journey
    and hungry for the bread of life.

    Only in the face of the child was the mouth so open;
    but aren't we all gasping for the bread of life?

    What is it that Jesus gives that we need?

    A meaning to life that is full,
    a love that somehow gives fullness.
    There's a lot of emptiness around,
    superficial meetings and the need for real love,
    selfish fantasies and the need for real fullness,
    various addictions and the need for real self-love;

    And don't we need to be like the child –
    not afraid to open the mouth,
    wide and spontaneous.

Just the open mouth said more than all the words,
a gesture which symbolised the world,
That's how we are before God.

Lord, I need to ask for the bread of life.

EIGHTEENTH SUNDAY IN ORDINARY TIME

I am the bread of life

>The bread that feeds the body:
>grown, harvested,
>baked, prepared
>by human hands;
>
>the bread of God,
>grown, harvested,
>baked, prepared
>by the hands of God and our hands.
>
>The bread of Jesus
>is the compassion of God for us, his people,
>the friendship and the forgiveness of God.
>
>The aroma of fresh bread can fill a house
>and the fragrance of God's presence fills our lives,
>especially when we most need it:
>
>the peace of God at times of death,
>the justice of God in hunger and homelessness,
>the closeness of God when we feel lonely.
>
>There could be no bread of life
>without our co-operation:
>And we bake that bread for the world;
>we are grateful for the gift of Jesus:
>for God's love in prayer
>and for the care of God
>experienced in the care of others.
>
>As we hear the words of Jesus:
>**I am the bread of life,**
>may we also say,
>with courage and thanks:
>we are the bread of life.

NINETEENTH SUNDAY IN ORDINARY TIME

Gift of God through others

> The wheat was sown in the land
> and grew silently, hidden, day and night;
> the wheat was harvested
> by many human hands.
> And bread was made:
> threshed, shaped, baked,
> and its fragrance filled the house.
>
> The fragrance of God
> is the air we breathe.
> The gifts of life and of love
> are the sources of human strength.
> And like the bread on the table,
> life and love come from God
> shaped and nurtured by human hands.
>
> The bread of life is the work of human hands;
> the work of Mary and Joseph caring for Jesus,
> the food made by them nourishing the son of God.
>
> The bread of life is Jesus,
> given to us by Mary, by God;
> given to us by many human hands,
> the hands that care for us in life.
>
> Jesus is the gift of God
> through many others
> to each of us.

TWENTIETH SUNDAY IN ORDINARY TIME

I give my flesh for the life of the world

>The promise of Jesus
>to give his flesh for the life of the world
>is the promise of someone
>who wants to give everything.
>
>Like the parent wanting to give everything –
>life, love, money, education,
>to the point when it hurts –
>Jesus wants to give himself,
>and the best way to do it now
>is to give his body.
>
>It's his way of saying:
>I want to give everything.
>
>We know what he means
>when we love someone,
>and our giving means it hurts ourselves.
>
>Where we suffer for another,
>we give our lives;
>where we suffer with another,
>we give our lives.
>Where we share the joy of another,
>we give our lives.
>
>What Jesus gives us,
>the bread and wine of his body and blood,
>is energy for growth,
>food for the journey,
>nourishment for the community,
>and we are, one and all,
>raised up, now and in the future.

For this bread of strength,
for this Eucharist of love,
we give thanks.

TWENTY-FIRST SUNDAY IN ORDINARY TIME

You have the message of eternal life

>We pick up messages
>about what will give us a full life,
>from many daily sources.
>
>We're told to seek the fullness of life
>in keeping the body young,
>or in knowing yourself,
>or in prayer and fasting,
>or in wealth and health,
>or in being well-insured.
>
>We're told to seek the fullness of life
>in avoiding pain,
>in doing good,
>in loving others.
>
>And Jesus says to seek the fullness of life,
>in knowing and living by the truths
>that God our Father loves us,
>that we are brothers and sisters,
>and that good overcomes evil.
>
>Jesus lived like this himself,
>aware of his Father's love,
>of his love for others,
>and courageous in his victory over evil.

TWENTY-SECOND SUNDAY IN ORDINARY TIME

The service of the heart

>The Lord looks on each of us
>and sees into our hearts.
>He sees within each of us
>the secrets and the richness
>that others often miss.
>He sees the whole person:
>what we do and fail to do,
>what we want to do,
>and the love we want to offer
>to others and to him.
>
>To God, many of our faults are seen as struggles,
>and many of our sins as mistakes.
>God sees what we would like to be,
>as much as what we are.
>And Jesus sees in each of us
>a brother and sister, child of God.
>
>And maybe it's true also
>that he sees the pride
>what may often be cloaked in generosity
>and the bits of selfishness cloaked in love,
>and he understands and forgives.
>
>The Lord wants us to honour him
>with the love of our hearts,
>not just the observance of religion;
>his desire for our faithful love
>encourages us in weakness
>and challenges us in strength.
>
>And he knows and loves in each of us
>what he knows and loves in Jesus.
>For he sees in us the image of his Son.

TWENTY-THIRD SUNDAY IN ORDINARY TIME

Bonded and free

A speech impediment
makes you afraid to meet people,
blocks you from saying what you want to say,
makes you feel inferior to others,
and you want to be healed, and free,
and that's what Jesus offered the one who came to him.

In many ways in life we are unfree,
and Jesus offers healing from our burdens,
like he healed the man with the stammer.

We fear what others think of us,
what they might say about us;
we fear we'll not be able to love forever,
and that another will not love us;
we fear illness and death,
and we fear we'll be left alone.

Jesus offers courage and freedom;
he unblocks our fears and anxieties;
he knows that we are capable of
love and forgiveness,
commitment and endurance
and his love grounds our confidence in ourselves.

He healed the speaker's impediment so that he could speak
    freely;
let him heal your impediments to love, to care, to live in joy
with the gift of his love and the example of
how he lived his life fully, lovingly and joyfully
in the face of suffering and of death.

TWENTY-FOURTH SUNDAY IN ORDINARY TIME

Thinking God's way

    Jesus died at the hands of violent people,
    and his disciples would have spared him
    or told him to live in such a way that
    no harm would come to him.
    But God's way was the way of love,
    the type of love that is proved in hardship,
    the type of love that is understood only in God.

    Illness for many years
    may seem like a waste to some;
    but we also see that within the illness
    was a strength that was life-giving to many,
    and through it a deep love and faith was born,
    even in times of hardship and frustration
    for a person who is ill and for carers.

    God's way is not to see illness,
    disability or confusion,
    failure or mistakes,
    as a waste,
    but as a way to love;
    for in the fragility of life we discover
    some of the deepest truths of human life.

    It is God's way to see the child of God in everyone,
    God's way to forgive and be reconciled,
    God's way to work for justice and peace,
    God's way to see, in the weakness of death,
    the strong promise of eternity.

    God sees no waste in life
    for in everything love can grow and God can be found.
    And that was the way for Jesus who said
    that the son of Man was to suffer grievously,

be put to death,
and on the third day rise again.

Jesus, once condemned to death,
now raised to life in the love of God.

TWENTY-FIFTH SUNDAY IN ORDINARY TIME

To be first with God

>To be first is a desire in many of us;
>first in class,
>first in sport,
>the favourite in the family,
>the favourite in the class;
>to be thought highly of,
>to be acclaimed.
>
>And that was the way with the disciples
>when they argued
>about which of them was the greatest.
>
>Maybe they argued about who was Jesus' favourite,
>or who was the leader of the group,
>or wanted to be seen as the closest to him
>by those who looked up to Jesus.
>
>We like honour and praise,
>we like prestige and to be looked up to,
>but the eyes of Jesus fell on a child
>when he wanted to say something
>about who was the greatest.
>
>When they all wondered
>how to be popular in the eyes of God,
>Jesus took a little child,
>and told us that when you welcome a child,
>you welcome God.
>
>To be first in the eyes of God
>is to be first in service,
>for the Son of man came
>not to be served but to serve.

TWENTY-SIXTH SUNDAY IN ORDINARY TIME

Remembered in the mind of God

What you give to others is received
into the hands and the heart of God
and is never forgotten.

The good we try to do and say –
all is remembered by God.

Help to a fellow-student in school or college,
a word of encouragement to a young person,
listening when someone needed your time,
all remembered in the mind of God.

Hours of being a loving parent,
love and care in your family,
time given for a friend in need,
the ordinary kindnesses of every day,
all remembered in the mind of God.

Creating jobs, giving employment,
talking and working for peace,
getting involved in the neighbourhood and parish,
all remembered in the mind of God.

The ways we help another to pray,
to make sense of faith,
and to get through bad times,
all remembered in the mind of God.

TWENTY-SEVENTH SUNDAY IN ORDINARY TIME

The love of children

> Jesus had a way with children,
> a welcome for them,
> a love for them,
> and saw in them
> some of the qualities of
> openness to God.
>
> The innocence of children and their weakness
> touch the strings of love in our hearts.
> If we are people of love,
> true followers of Jesus,
> we will want the best for our children.
>
> We want happiness and love for them,
> good health and a meaning in their lives,
> we want them to find friends.
> We want to spare them the hardships of life,
> and when we cannot,
> we want to give them a light to guide them
> in what will be the pain of life.
>
> We hope also to give them a way through
> the inevitable difficulties
> of love and of growth which they will find
> as they make their way through life.
>
> Can we give them
> the way of Jesus?
>
> He had a way with children
> because he is the Way to God.

TWENTY-EIGHTH SUNDAY IN ORDINARY TIME

Costing no less than everything

Sometimes love costs no less than everything.

Parents knows this
in bringing up children in love;
and then it costs a lot to let them go,
as they make their way through life,
finding their own feet,
forming their own families.

And the love of God opens the door
to people who are poor;
if we fail to recognise the poor in our world
we are missing God.

And we know that a passion for wealth
can close us off from other people
as we fail to see their needs
and get into competition with them.

The call of the Lord is
to give of ourselves for others,
even when it hurts;
and into a love which shares
with those who are poor.
His love calls us,
and when we live in this love
of giving and receiving,
we are the most blessed of people.

TWENTY-NINTH SUNDAY IN ORDINARY TIME

Not to be served, but to serve

What we remember most in anyone's life,
is not so much what they achieved,
but the love in which they lived.

Jesus himself is remembered more for his death
out of love for all his people
than for any great achievements.

He wrote no music or symphony,
but shared the song of God's love;
he painted no great masterpiece,
but showed us we are all God's work of art;
wrote no great book,
but his words of comfort and love
resound through all our joys and sorrows.

He has shown us what the Son of man is capable of
when he lives in the shadows and light of God;
and he has shown us what every man and woman
can be guided towards.

Sitting at the right and the left of Jesus –
that's language he doesn't go for.
To live and grow, to suffer and struggle
in love of self and others,
is the way to glory in the sight of God,
and this is the only glory worth our effort.

THIRTIETH SUNDAY IN ORDINARY TIME

Let me see again

    In the varied colours of the hills,
    the changing sound of waves,
    the steady flow of rivers
    let me see, Lord God, your beauty,
    your peace, your eternity.

    In the care of friendship,
    the love of family,
    the commitment of husband and wife,
    let me see, Lord God, your love,
    your care, your faithfulness.

    In care for the poor,
    commitment of justice,
    in work for peace,
    let me see, Lord God, your passion
    your care for the poor, your Incarnation.

    In joy and in laughter,
    may I see your joy.
    In suffering and in mourning,
    let me see your cross.
    In forgiveness and in courage,
    let me see your resurrection.

Let me see again.

THIRTY-FIRST SUNDAY IN ORDINARY TIME

Not far from the Kingdom of God

    Words we connect with the Kingdom of God,
    like gentle, kind,
    compassionate, caring,
    are words we connect with Jesus.

    Activities like working for justice,
    caring for the poor,
    housing the homeless,
    concern for the developing world,
    teaching prayer and the meaning of life,
    are activities within the Kingdom of God.

    We want to be like Jesus,
    accepting of others
    in difficulty and dispute,
    forgiving of faults and failings,
    challenging in teaching the truth,
    for he is the human image of
    the kingdom of God,
    and when you try to live like him,
    you are not far from the Kingdom of God.

    These are some words and activities of love,
    For to love God and the neighbour
    means you are not far from the Kingdom of God.

    This is our entry to God's Kingdom.

THIRTY-SECOND SUNDAY IN ORDINARY TIME

We are never too poor to give to God

In the times of our lives
when we feel weak and discouraged,
we feel we have little to give to God –
or to others.

After failing an exam, losing a job,
finding out we are very ill or near to death,
when love has gone wrong
or our children have turned to crime,
we may feel we have little to offer.

He looks on us,
like a mother looks on a child
who is making awkward efforts to help her.
As he praised the poor woman,
for her contribution to the temple,

Jesus, like God our Father,
sees the intentions of the heart,
and values what we offer.

Like the snow melts into a river
and every small flake is part of the river,
so all we give from the heart
becomes part of the big love of God.

We are never too poor to give to God,
for what God likes
is the gift of the heart.

THIRTY-THIRD SUNDAY IN ORDINARY TIME

My words will not pass away

> Some things last in life:
> like love and compassion,
> memory of kindnesses, big and small,
> influence of parents on children,
> moments of love, friendship and compassion,
> remembered and relived even when people have passed on.
>
> And the word of God lasts,
> even though the heavens and earth
> the weather and the winds,
> the crops and the plants,
> change each day and season.
>
> The pictures Jesus uses are frightening:
> stars falling and the moon darkening,
> the sun going cold and dark.
>
> We fear the upheaval of the earth,
> like turbulence on a plane flight,
> like thunder and lightening,
> like an earthquake moving our furniture.
>
> We presume the earth will last forever,
> and Jesus is saying that
> his word is more lasting than the universe.
>
> And we fear the signs he mentions:
> but these are not to be frightening signs,
> just signs that God is near.
>
> Everything we see and experience,
> turbulent and calm, joyful and sad,
> can be to the eye of faith,
> a sign of the nearness of God.

LAST SUNDAY IN ORDINARY TIME
CHRIST THE KING

Mine is not a kingdom of this world

> Many voices direct our lives:
> voices which direct to wealth and comfort,
> or to relationships which do not last,
> voices for peace and for justice,
> and the voices we tune into in prayer.
>
> Voices speaking of violence and power,
> and others of compassion and forgiveness;
> voices which call us back to another era
> when things now seem better than they were then.
>
> And the voice of Jesus.
> The voice which appeals for peace and justice
> in a world often proposing violence and greed;
> the voice which is strong for forgiveness
> when our own hearts are bitter;
> the voice which speaks the truth
> that is fully human and is the word of God.
>
> His Kingdom is not of this world,
> but is part of this world;
> like the branch is part of the tree.
> And when we speak of justice, peace,
> forgiveness and love,
> we speak of his Kingdom;
> and when we live from his truth,
> we are not far from the Kingdom of God.

THE IMMACULATE CONCEPTION

Privileged at birth

>Mary is praised with many titles,
>*Immaculate Conception* is one of them,
>and often we don't know their full meaning.
>
>Her names of praise are remembered
>because she was the mother of Jesus,
>and lived through her life
>the love and call of God
>in a way that was unusual.
>
>A woman of faith who believed
>that her son was God when he was dying on the cross;
>a woman of trust
>who believed in God's promise to her
>even when Jesus seemed the weakest of human beings;
>a woman of hope
>as she carried her dead Son's body to the tomb.
>
>And who was not surprised when he appeared to her later,
>for she believed that he would rise from death
>as God had promised and Jesus had said,
>though she might not have known how he would rise.
>
>Mary, girl and woman
>of faith which gave her roots,
>of hope which gave her courage,
>of love which made life worthwhile.
>
>Because of the depth
>of her faith and hope,
>and the brightness of love in her soul,
>we know that at the moment of birth
>she was privileged with grace
>and we can say Immaculate Conception.

THE EPIPHANY OF THE LORD

Follow your star

    Three wise people
    following a star,
    not always asking
    nor did they know,
    where it came from,
    nor where it would lead them.

    Follow your star:
    many voices tell us that.

    The star of wealth, of success,
    the star of popularity, prestige.
    What is your star?
    The star of love, of faith,
    the star which lights up the needs of others,
    what stars do you follow?

    If the star leads to God,
    it will lead to love, compassion,
    and, like the wise people,
    it will fill us with delight.

    Sometimes dim, sometimes clear,
    sometimes behind a cloud,
    or lost in the light of other stars,
    the star of God
    is the word of Jesus,
    the forgiveness of the Spirit,
    the Bread of Life,
    and the star gives light,
    and beckons us further on the journey of God
    in the way of Jesus.

We may follow other paths,
other ways.
Different Herods may suggest
that we travel by other stars,
losing God's direction.

May the brightness of
love, justice,
truth and meaning
be the environment in which we live.

And may the way we live
on the journey in the starlight,
be a light for those
who share our life's journey.

Do not try too hard to understand your star:
be content to have found a star in life,
and know that it is from God and will lead you to God.

SAINT PATRICK

No longer an outsider

    Patrick might have been called an outsider,
the stranger who came from another land,
a man away from home,
the prisoner on the winter mountain.

The outsider went deeper inside himself.
The stranger found the companionship of God,
and the prisoner of the northern mountain found the
    freedom of God.
Outsider, prisoner, stranger,
he found God, he found his mission
and he found his happiness.

That's the way of many people.
Our people have often been outsiders.
But if you seek God,
and when you live in the life of God,
you're never on the outside,
never a prisoner,
never a stranger.

Patrick lived on the inside.
Inside the heart of God.
And there he found the big meaning of his life,
and there he found a new home, a new people.

In the depths of his faith, his loneliness
and his desire to spread the gospel of Jesus,
he found within himself the holy well,
and there he found God and peace,
and the call to work for the kingdom of God,
no longer prisoner, outsider or stranger.

That's what we need.
To find that within ourselves the holy well
where God is loving and calling us.

In that holy well we find
that inside all of us
is the God who loves us,
walks with us in life,
climbs our mountains and
descends into all our wells
so that everything is a holy mountain and a holy well.

There are no outsiders,
only the people of God, called, loved,
and brothers and sisters in Jesus Christ.

THE ASCENSION OF THE LORD

The way, truth and life

    Risen Lord,
    Be the way that guides my steps,
    be the truth that enlightens my mind,
    be the life that gives love to my heart.

    Be the way:
    the sure path on ground even or uneven,
    on the straight or turning road,
    the narrow or the wide.
    The path of life bears your footprints.
    Share it with me.
    You are the way
    to truth, to life, to heaven.

    Be the truth:
    the golden string in uncertainty,
    glimpsed or fully known.
    The meaning of life bears your word.
    Share it with us.
    You are the truth
    on the way, of life, about heaven.

    Be the life:
    the hope and optimism in love,
    the third in every friendship.
    All love bears your life.
    Share it, Lord Jesus.
    You are the life,
    on our way, in the truth, forever in heaven.

THE BODY AND BLOOD OF CHRIST

Nourishment and energy for the journey

In our hunger for love,
God offers the nourishment
of his love for us;
a love which is total,
the total acceptance
that each of us yearns for.

In our hunger for wholeness,
wanting to know we are forgiven,
God offers the nourishment of forgiveness,
inviting us to leave the past
where it best belongs –
in his compassionate heart.

In our hunger for meaning,
God offers the nourishment
of the word and life of Jesus,
and we know, in all our confusion,
that we are not lost.

And in our desire to do good,
to create a better world for people,
to live in the cause of justice and peace,
God offers energy and new hope.
We know he is on our side,
and we work, not on our own,
but with him.

In our desire to live in love,
forgiveness and reconciliation,
he offers the energy of his risen Son,
and in our hopes to care for those we love,
children and family,
friends and the poor,

he offers energy,
from our friendship with Jesus.

In the Bread of life, the body of Christ,
God gives food for the journey.
In the Wine of life, the blood of Christ,
God gives energy for the journey.

As we eat this food and drink this wine,
we know we never walk alone.

THE ASSUMPTION OF MARY

Mary was someone who knew death close at hand

She turned to God for help
as all of us do in bereavement,
when her husband died.
She knew the death of mother and father,
and the support of cousins and relations
at a time of mourning.

She would pray often
as we pray ourselves at times of loss,
He has come to my help,
mindful of his mercy.

Did she not ponder the mystery of life and death,
seeking consolation and comfort in loneliness
like any woman and man, like ourselves?

One of us in life,
she is now alive with God,
as we shall be in eternity.

At the cross she heard the words of Jesus,
giving her as mother to another.
She seemed to lose her son totally on the cross;
she lost him to violence and to pain
as he died for the life of the world.

She believed that he would rise;
but she did not know how or when.
Her faith was her comfort,
as Jesus gave up his spirit.

She was no stranger to death;
and she was blessed,
graced by God,
in her mourning.

She knew that death was not final,
and lived her life in the air of eternity,
having welcomed the Son of heaven into her womb.

In Mary eternity joined earth in the closest possible
    bond;
in Mary earth has joined eternity,
as she now enjoys the presence of God,
body and soul in the life of God.

As she was on earth, we also are called to be:
carriers of God in our own lives;
as she is in heaven, we one day shall be,
as God carries us in his arms,
welcoming us home
into our eternal home.

ALL SAINTS

God's work of art

> We are all different,
> all unique,
> all God's work of art.
>
> We remember today
> all our saints,
> all the human race
> who have reached God.
> Each person,
> man or woman,
> young or old,
> mirrors something of the face of God.
>
> And there is a common thread which unites us all:
> our need for love and community,
> for home and acceptance,
> for love, respect, forgiveness.
>
> And the need to love:
> the desire to make this world a better place,
> to create with God
> a world of justice, love and peace.
>
> Because the world is full of people,
> it is charged with the grandeur of God.
>
> We look at everyone and listen to them,
> and see and hear in them
> the glory of God.
>
> The feast of All Saints honours us all,
> living and dead.
> The feast celebrates those gone before us
> and proclaims with love

that the finest common thread among us
is that we are children of God,
friends of Jesus Christ
and the place where God's glory dwells.